Kristallnacht

Jude   Jude

PERSPECTIVES ON

Kristallnacht

Nazi Persecution of the Jews in Europe

WIL MARA

Marshall Cavendish
Benchmark
New York

This book is dedicated to Dr. Steven J. Goldstein, with much gratitude.

Marshall Cavendish Benchmark
99 White Plains Road
Tarrytown, NY 10591-5502
www.marshallcavendish.us

Expert Reader: Dr. Dennis Klein, Professor of History and Director, Jewish
Studies Program, Kean University, Union, New Jersey

Library of Congress Cataloging-in-Publication Data

Mara, Wil
Kristallnacht : Nazi Persecution of the Jews in Europe / by Wil Mara.
p. cm. — (Perspectives on)
Includes bibliographical references and index.
Summary: "Provides comprehensive information on the persecution of Jews
in Europe commencing in 1938 and its legacy"—Provided by publisher.
ISBN 978-0-7614-4026-0
1. Jews—Persecutions—Germany—Juvenile literature. 2. Kristallnacht,
1938—Juvenile literature. 3. Antisemitism—Germany—History—20th century—
Juvenile literature. 4. Holocaust, Jewish (1939–1945)—Juvenile literature. I. Title.
DS134.255.M37 2009
940.53'1842—dc22
2008042971

Editor: Christine Florie
Publisher: Michelle Bisson
Art Director: Anahid Hamparian
Series Designer: Sonia Chaghatzbanian

Photo research by Marybeth Kavanagh

Cover photo by Fred Ramage/Keystone Features/Getty Images

The photographs in this book are used by permission and through the courtesy of:
AP Photo: 2–3; *Getty Images*: New York Times Co., 8; Time Life Pictures/US Army
Signal Corps, 11; Hulton Archive, 16, 21, 39; Keystone, 53, 68; Fred Ramage, 64,
70; Imagno, 59; Gerard Malie/AFP, 94; *Corbis*: 82; Bettmann, 19, 57; Austrian
Archives, 61; dpa, 76; *The Granger Collection*: 54; ullstein bild, 24, 36, 80; *The Image
Works*: akg-images, 34, 41, 43; Mary Evans Picture Library, 92

Printed in Malaysia
1 3 5 6 4 2

Contents

Introduction

PERSECUTION OF OTHERS ON THE BASIS of race and/or religion is nothing new to humanity. Since the earliest recorded times, people have found countless ways to suspect, resent, disdain, dislike, and attack those of differing ethnicities or beliefs. For the most part this has manifested itself in relatively minor fashion — the cruel thought, the insensitive comment, or the distasteful joke. Some take it a step further and vow to avoid meaningful interaction with those they consider beneath them.

The next level goes beyond the passive and into the aggressive — refusal to hire certain people at a company, serve them at a restaurant, or permit them to join a social club or other organization. There are threatening phone calls and letters, attacks on property, and then, most viciously, attacks on the people themselves. History is littered with grim tales of ethnic and religious groups being targeted. From the Indian caste system to the persecution of Christians under the rule of the Roman emperor Diocletian to the enslavement of Africans in North America, humans have subjugated and violated the rights of their fellow humans due to their ethnic or religious heritage again and again.

The Nazi atrocities against the Jews of Europe are remarkable for several reasons. First, the man who led the effort—the German führer Adolf Hitler—made his feelings toward the Jews very clear long before he came into power. He wrote and published a book called *Mein Kampf* (*My Struggle*) that includes sections spelling out his hatred for the Jewish people and his belief that they were to blame for the ills of the world. In spite of this, he and his National Socialist German Workers' Party (i.e., Nazis) rose in popularity in the 1930s, enabling him to build a power base and eventually become Germany's leader. He acted upon his hatred of Jews first by promulgating laws that stripped them of their citizenship and their dignity, then by staging outright attacks against them. In early November 1938 these attacks began with the event known as Kristallnacht, which in English means "crystal night," although the more commonly used translation is the Night of Broken Glass. As it turned out, Kristallnacht was just a hint of what was to come, as Hitler launched a plan to permanently remove Jews from all of Europe soon thereafter.

How was this allowed to happen? How did a man with such callous ambitions reach the top of the political ladder? Did the rest of the German people know what was going on? If so, how did the average German citizen feel about it? Did non-Jews take any action against Hitler and his Nazi followers? And what about the governments and people of other nations? What was their reaction? Did those in power step in to try to put an end to Hitler's plans? Did they act out of conscience or common decency, or did they stand by while others endured unimaginable suffering?

Kristallnacht and the horrors that followed forever changed the course of history. And therefore we must investigate, from all perspectives, exactly what happened before, during, and after November 9–10, 1938.

One

Setting the Stage

KRISTALLNACHT MAY NOT HAVE OCCURRED until late 1938, but the social and political conditions that made it possible began developing long before then. Incidents like this are never truly isolated; history has shown that the mind-set of certain people has to be in the right place.

World War I and Nationalistic Pride

Throughout the nineteenth century, Europe was the political, economic, military, and cultural heartbeat of the world. This was sustained for such a long period in part because of the region's ability to avoid major internal conflicts. There were small skirmishes from time to time, but nothing that threatened Europe's position as the leader of the global community.

That began to change with the onset of extreme nationalism—fervent, almost irrational pride in one's home country. It fostered a sense of competitiveness between European nations that brought about the desire for the stronger of them to control the weaker. At the same time, many of these

As nationalistic pride took hold in twentieth-century Europe, Germany built up its military.

weaker nations were looking to cast off the chains of colonialism and enjoy the benefits of independence. Tensions rose as one country after another began building up its armed forces in a quest for military dominance, and the once-admirable sense of European brotherhood began to deteriorate.

By the start of the twentieth century Germany had established itself as continental Europe's premier military presence. It had the best-trained army and an increasingly powerful navy. Prior to this, the finest navy belonged to the nearby island nation of the United Kingdom, which was understandably nervous about Germany's growing shadow. Soon, uneasy alliances began to form—one European nation would join with another to ensure that it wouldn't be overrun by a third, but then the third joined with a fourth to become more formidable than the first two, and so on. By the early 1910s tensions had risen to an unbearable degree.

The match that finally lit the fuse igniting World War I was the assassination of Archduke Franz Ferdinand of Austria-Hungary. Ferdinand, an heir to Austria-Hungary's throne, hoped to reduce some of the bad feelings that had gripped Europe. On June 28, 1914, however, a Serbian terrorist seeking independence for his homeland from Austria-Hungary shot and killed both Ferdinand and his wife, Sophie, as they drove through Sarajevo. One month later Austria-Hungary, with Germany's full support, declared war on Serbia. It didn't take long for other European nations to get involved—choosing either the side of the Central Powers, led by Austria-Hungary and Germany, or the Allied Powers, led by France, Russia, and the United Kingdom (all concerned about Germany's military might and in support of an independent Serbia)—and World War I was under way.

Known at the time as the Great War, it would last until November 1918 and involve nearly every country in the world. In the end the Allied Powers were victorious, due in large part to the involvement of the United States in April 1917. President Woodrow Wilson declared war on Germany after Germany attacked several unarmed American vessels, tried to cut off supplies that the United States was sending to Allied forces, and invited Mexico to wage attacks on U.S. soil on Germany's behalf.

Soldiers celebrate the end of World War I and the victory of the Allied Powers.

The cost of World War I in all respects was enormous. More than 10 million people lost their lives, and at least another 21 million people were injured. Much of this was due to the development of new weapons technology, capable of causing greater destruction than ever before. In terms of financial costs the combined spending for all nations reached well over $300 billion—a staggering sum in 1918. Entire cities were left in ruins, making it difficult for survivors of the war to find food and clean water, much less a job or a place to live. And politically the European nations paid a heavy price—due to their hobbled economies, new opportunities arose for the United States around the world, shifting the global power structure for the first time in centuries. Europe still held a place of importance, but its status had been severely diminished by the ravages of war.

In the aftermath of World War I, leaders from both sides met in January 1919 to draw up a formal peace agreement. President Wilson hoped it would be a reasonably amicable affair, but the European victors had other intentions. With so much of their land ravaged, so many of their citizens dead, and so much of their power and influence around the world greatly reduced, they saw the meeting as an opportunity to exact revenge. Germany, in particular, was singled out for the harshest punishment—each vanquished nation was required to sign an individual treaty, and the one for Germany, known as the Treaty of Versailles, levied the most crushing terms. Germany had to relinquish control of many of its colonies, some of which provided resources essential to the nation's well-being. The nation was also required to pay financial reparations for the damage done to Allied lands. And it had to reduce its armed forces to a fraction of its former might. But perhaps the most humiliating term in the treaty was that Germany had to publicly accept complete responsibility for the war—an international slap in the face.

Germany suffered for years following the Treaty of Versailles. The proud and once-powerful nation was brought to its knees, where it remained mired in hardship and economic stagnation. It was understandable, then, that the people of Germany grew to resent their predicament, the European neighbors who put them in it, and their own military decisions of the past. When German leadership failed to remedy the situation, the people became frustrated and desperate, and they called for change. For one ambitious young politician this was the opportunity he'd been waiting for.

Rise of a Dictator

Adolf Hitler was born in Austria on April 20, 1889. His father, Alois, was a fifty-one-year-old government employee, and his mother, twenty-eight-year-old Klara, was a housewife. Hitler had a difficult childhood that included frequent beatings by his hot-tempered father. He began displaying the same violent tendencies at an early age, often hitting his siblings and bullying his schoolmates.

He was a good student in his early years, but his grades sagged later on. After his father died, in 1903, he left secondary school without a diploma. His ambition was to be an artist. In 1907 he move to Vienna to attend the prestigious Academy of Fine Arts but failed the entrance examination in both 1907 and 1908. He made some money selling drawings and paintings, but he lived mostly off money he inherited from his late mother, who had died a few years after his father. He also considered pursuing a career in architecture but ultimately decided he didn't have enough formal education.

It was during this period that Hitler began to develop an interest in politics. Although born in Austria, he spoke High German and considered himself a German at heart. (He would later acquire full German citizenship.) He became intensely proud of his adopted country, developing the same kind of fierce national pride that was sweeping through Europe at the time. It is likely that this is when he began theorizing ways to improve Germany's situation. One crucial step, he decided, was to cleanse it of undesirables—people who didn't measure up to what he felt was the natural superiority of the German "race." And the leading class of undesirables, in his opinion, was the Jews. He would later write,

> It was not until I was fourteen or fifteen
> years old that I frequently ran up against
> the word "Jew," partly in connection with
> political controversies. These references
> aroused a slight aversion in me, and I could
> not avoid an uncomfortable feeling which
> always came over me when I had to listen
> to religious disputes.

There was a great deal of anti-Semitism (i.e., contempt toward Jews) in Viennese society at the time, and he absorbed it diligently. He was exposed to common anti-Semitic ideas such as the notion that Jews were the leaders of socialist and communist movements that brought Germany to ruin following World War I; Jews were subversively in cooperation with anti-German leaders in other nations; Jews led comfortable lives during Germany's economic depression while other

Martin Luther and His Dirty Little Book

Many historians believe that some of the anti-Semitism prevalent in Germany and Austria during Hitler's youth was caused by a relatively small publication that was, at that time, already almost four hundred years old—*The Jews and Their Lies*, written by the German Reformation leader Martin Luther. Luther was angry with the Jewish community for failing to embrace his movement—a Christian alternative to Catholicism. Containing lines such as "[Jews] must be accounted as filth," and "They should be shown no mercy or kindness, afforded no legal protection . . . [and] drafted into forced labor or expelled for all time," the book's sentiment certainly anticipated the actions of the Nazi Party years later. Copies were handed out at Nazi rallies, given as gifts among members, and quoted in Nazi-run newspapers.

German citizens suffered; and Jews controlled and manipulated Germanic society by holding key positions in everything from mass media to the banking industry. By the time he left Vienna in 1913, Hitler's hatred of the Jewish community was in full bloom.

When World War I broke out in 1914, Hitler became part of a Bavarian military unit. He accepted several extremely dangerous assignments and went on to win several decorations for bravery. In spite of this he never rose higher than

During World War I Adolf Hitler fought the Allies in a Bavarian unit, rising only to the rank of corporal.

the rank of corporal. In 1918 he was temporarily blinded by mustard gas and sent to a military hospital. While there, the war came to an end. Hitler joined others of his generation who were crushed by the thought that their beloved Germany had been defeated, then further humiliated by the Treaty of Versailles. In his mind the Jews were to blame for all of it. He believed, for example, that wealthy Jews blocked the flow of money to the military that was needed to win the war effort. He thought Jewish businessmen who were selling arms and other needed goods may have been providing them to both Germany and the nations it was fighting. Similarly, Jewish businessmen who were treating their workers unfairly may have been the cause of several strikes that occurred, which in turn drove down the production of war materials during crucial times in the military campaign. Jews who ran popular newspapers, he felt, were often too critical of Germany in their editorials and other articles. Hitler also thought Jews were largely behind the promotion of communism, which was contrary to Germany's core political philosophies. This suspicion was only exacerbated by incidents like the temporary takeover of the Bavarian city of Munich following the war by a group called the Bavarian Socialist Republic—a communist faction that had several Jewish leaders.

Hitler formally entered politics in 1919, when he became the spokesman for the National Socialist German Workers' Party, also known as the Nazis. The Nazi Party shared many of Hitler's views, including fervent nationalism and fierce anti-Semitism. The average Nazi also harbored lingering resentments toward the German surrender in World War I, the smothering conditions of the Versailles Treaty, and the ineffectiveness of the ensuing German leadership.

Hitler's prominence within the Nazi Party increased quickly. Colleagues were in awe of his passion for the party's mandate, his ability to recruit new members, and—perhaps most important—his mesmerizing oratorical skills. In 1923, with Germany suffering economic ruin and widespread civil unrest, he tried to lead the Nazis into overthrowing the German government in a coup that came to be called the Beer Hall Putsch. The attempt failed, and Hitler was sent to prison.

While in prison he wrote *Mein Kampf*, in which he outlined his opinion that German people were superior to all others, that Jews had to be systematically eliminated, and that the German empire could rise again through military might and the conquering of other nations. Hitler was released from prison the following year and saw to it that *Mein Kampf* was published. During this period of frustration and bitterness felt by the German people, it eventually sold hundreds of thousands of copies throughout the country—a sign to Hitler that the Nazis and their ideas were beginning to take root. A bone-chilling passage from *Mein Kampf* reads:

> What soon gave me cause for very serious consideration were the activities of the Jews in certain branches of life, into the mystery of which I penetrated little by little. Was there any shady undertaking, any form of foulness, especially in cultural life, in which at least one Jew did not participate? On putting the probing knife carefully to that kind of abscess one immediately discovered, like a maggot in a putrescent body, a little Jew who was often blinded by the sudden light.

In 1929 the Great Depression—the most severe economic crash in modern history—struck like a thunderbolt, first in the United States and then the rest of the world. The situation in Germany, which was dire already, became even worse, and Germany's citizens demanded change. Hitler used this unfortunate turn of events to further trumpet his Nazi Party. He talked of simple, effective solutions, while other political organizations became bogged down in bureaucracy, lethargy, and internal strife. He extolled Germany's essential greatness. As a result, the Nazis won major election victories

As a result of Hitler's prominence in the Nazi Party, Germany's president Paul von Hindenburg (right) had no choice but to appoint him chancellor.

in 1932. Hitler appealed to German president Paul von Hindenburg to appoint him Germany's new chancellor (head of a parliamentary government or cabinet). After his appointment, he also persuaded Hindenburg to agree to legislation that stripped power from those for whom Hitler had no use. By the time Hindenburg died in August 1934, Hitler, the former Bavarian corporal and high school dropout, was in complete control of the German government.

The Nightmare Begins

Just as Hitler wasted no time reshaping the government in order to consolidate his power, he acted almost immediately to manifest his feelings toward the Jewish people and others. It should be noted that Hitler was not alone in his crusade to "cleanse" German society, nor could the crusade have been carried out without the help of others. Hitler may have been the leader of Germany, but there were hundreds around him, from high-ranking civil servants to powerful military officers, who had long held manifold prejudices of their own. They were only too happy to help rid the nation of "undesirables" while gaining Hitler's approval to further their careers.

In April 1933, for example, there was a temporary boycott of all shops and markets owned by Jews. Members of Hitler's private army—known formally as the Sturm Abteilung (SA) and in English called the Storm Troopers—blocked the entrances to these businesses, harassing and even beating those who tried to pass through. Hitler also enacted more than forty new laws aimed at limiting the citizenship of German Jews, making it essentially illegal to be Jewish.

In April 1933 members of the SA posted notices on Jewish storefronts urging Germans to boycott them.

One of these laws forbade Jews from holding government positions of any kind. This also cleared the path for Hitler to dismiss all Jewish teachers, including noted and respected scholars working in Germany's universities, because

Racism for All

Hitler and his followers focused much of their hatred on Jews—but not on Jews exclusively. The Nazis considered nearly everyone who wasn't "Aryan stock" to be a threat to Germany's future. Along with the millions of Jews who would be targeted in the years ahead, the Nazis would also work to rid the nation of all handicapped people (both mentally and physically), prostitutes, homosexuals, alcoholics and drug addicts, Slavs, Sinti and Roma (gypsies), Jehovah's Witnesses, and others. In short, anyone who didn't measure up—or in some cases were simply disliked by Hitler or his subordinates—eventually became victims of the purge. Jews, however, would be singled out for the greatest hostility, largely due to their perceived power within German society. This made them the most convenient scapegoats for Hitler's wrath and their mistreatment the foundation upon which he built his influence over the German people.

they were considered civil servants. Other areas in which Jews were not permitted to pursue careers included law, journalism, and medicine.

A few foreign nations reached out to these displaced professionals, offering financial assistance and, in some cases, citizenship as well as new positions. But most did nothing, nor did most non-Jewish German citizens. There were a handful of demonstrations around Germany protesting Hitler's policies, but nothing of consequence.

Facing such feeble opposition, Hitler enacted nineteen new anti-Jewish laws in 1934 and almost thirty more in 1935. The 1935 collection was perhaps the most direct because it dealt specifically with the definition—at least by Hitler's standards—of who was a Jew versus a "true" German. This led to the Nuremberg Laws, so named because they were announced in September 1935 during a Nazi rally in the southwestern city of Nuremburg. There were two parts to the Nuremburg Laws, which would become the foundation for many of Hitler's anti-Jewish policies and practices to come: the Law for the Protection of German Blood and Honor and the Reich Citizenship Law. The former outlawed marriages and even sexual intercourse between Jews and "true" Germans, and the latter no longer recognized Jews as citizens, even if their families had lived in Germany for centuries. Also in 1935 the Nazis moved beyond mere legislation and began openly attacking Jews on a regular basis. This included more boycotts (although there was a lull from 1936 to 1938), assaults both public and private, and the theft of Jewish property. While the attacks may not have been as frequent or as widespread as Hitler may have wished

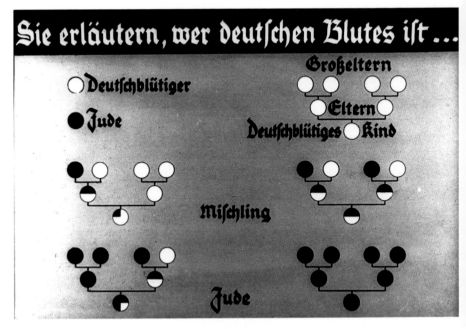

A training course for Hitler Youth in 1935 included a lecture on the evils of racial mixing between German Aryans (white cells) and Jews (black cells).

(and why more Jews didn't flee the country immediately), they were a sure sign of things to come.

The Devastating Effect of Silence

By the time the Nuremburg Laws were promulgated, it was clear that Hitler was capable of driving the entire Jewish presence out of Germany. It's hard to imagine that anyone with a conscience could stand by while this was happening—common moral certitude all but demanded that such flagrant disregard for civil rights be met with coordinated resistance. Jews made up less than 1 percent of the German population at the time, yet Hitler was blaming them for all of Germany's ills and taking steps to eliminate them. Would anyone oppose this behavior?

A few dared to try. For example, after a group of Jewish men were savagely beaten (two to death) by Storm Troopers in the southwestern town of Niederstetten in March 1933, a local Lutheran pastor condemned the attacks during a speech to his congregation. He was attacked shortly thereafter, which sent a clear message that a person would be targeted if he or she displayed any sympathy toward Jews. (Shortly after the beating, the pastor developed such intense anxiety from the fear that his wife and four daughters would also be attacked that he committed suicide.)

In spite of such retaliatory threats, others still had the courage to act. One was a pastor named Heinrich Gruber. Working from a Protestant church in the German capital of Berlin—the epicenter of the Nazi movement—Gruber regularly criticized Hitler's anti-Semitic policies to his congregation and provided escape routes for Jews into neighboring Holland. He was captured by the Gestapo—Hitler's secret police—in 1940, after helping thousands of Jews avoid persecution. Another brave individual was Countess Maria von Maltzan, who had been born into a wealthy family and had a brother in Hitler's Schutzstaffel (SS)—the "Protective Battalion," or ultra-elite protective guard similar to America's Secret Service—and therefore had access to high-ranking Nazi officials. At the risk of severe punishment and even death, she regularly hid Jewish refugees in her own home, fed them, forged official documents so they could leave the country, and sometimes personally drove them into safe territory.

The Reichsvertretung

Not long after Hitler came to power and began enacting anti-Semitic laws, Jews in western Germany spearheaded the formation of an organization to represent Jewish interests on a national level. This became known as the Reichsvertretung—the Reich Deputation of German Jews. Its goal—admirable in purpose but, as time would tell, somewhat futile—was to provide assistance to German Jews who found life under Hitler's regime difficult and unpleasant. This included professional retraining for those who had lost their jobs as a result of Nazi laws, education for children who had been forced out of state-run German schools, economic assistance and basic necessities for those left homeless, and preparation and paperwork for those who wanted to emigrate. In spite of the increasing harassment of Jews as the 1930s wore on, men and women held their posts in the Reichsvertretung, working to aid those in need. One such individual, Otto Hirsch, was an attorney with a bright personality, a charming sense of humor, and the courage to face off with Nazi officials. One author who knew him well remembered, "In tireless effort, always ready to help, always ready to listen to people, he carried on for years the work of the Reichsvertretung. He never lost his courage." In 1941 the Nazis arrested him and sent him to the Mauthausen concentration camp, where he was tortured to death.

Many German Jews tried to help themselves simply by leaving the country. For the most part Hitler's Nazi government was only too happy to let them go. However, they would often strip Jewish families of their belongings before doing so; seizing a home and its contents was not unusual. Often a family was permitted to take only one suitcase per person, while everything else became the property of the Third Reich (another name for Hitler's Nazi regime; *reich* literally means "empire" in German). A few foreign nations aided the exiting Jews by granting citizenship to a certain number at a time. The United States, Great Britain, and Palestine accepted tens of thousands of Jewish immigrants during this period. They still set limits, though, which meant thousands more had to remain within Germany's hostile borders.

In spite of the charity of these nations, plus the brave actions of such people as Heinrich Gruber and Maria von Maltzan, the great majority of individuals did little or nothing to combat Hitler's racist rampage. Some German citizens voluntarily turned a blind eye to it. They were more concerned with getting the nation back on its feet in terms of economy, industry, and international power and therefore considered the "Jewish issue" to be of relatively little importance. After experiencing years of hardship, they were simply thankful that they had a new leader who was creating jobs, building roads, and providing food. Melita Maschmann, a follower of Hitler living a few miles outside of Berlin, remembered her willingness to accept the Nazis' condemnation of the Jews: "I said to myself: the Jews are the enemies of the New Germany. . . . If the Jews sow hatred against us all over the world, they must learn that we have hostages for them in our hands." It was her way of rationalizing Nazi behavior. Similarly, there was a segment of German society that fully agreed with Hitler's attitude that the elimination of Jews was a necessary step toward the purification of the German populace. Hitler played upon the deep-rooted hatred of Jews by many Germans who had long labored under the impression that the removal of Jews and other undesirable groups was the central step to German supremacy and an ideal, nearly perfect German society. For these people the easiest reaction to Hitler's brutality was simply to pretend they didn't see it—and thousands took this approach.

Other nations may have publicly condemned Hitler's anti-Semitic actions, but they took no steps to actively stop him. They still had to deal with him in terms of trade and commerce. Disregarding the terms of the Treaty of Versailles, Hitler began rebuilding Germany's military while employing thousands in munitions factories. Much of Europe was bogged down in the Great Depression and, as Hitler well knew, in no position to wage another war or to try to stop the military buildup. The more he got away with, the bolder he became. Once his armies were ready, he began sending troops into France and Spain, then annexed his home country of Austria.

In mid-1938 Hitler set his sights on conquering Czechoslovakia, and by autumn he had an invasion plan in place. England and France reluctantly began preparing their troops to defend their Czechoslovakian allies. But then they decided—foolishly, as history would later illustrate—to make a deal with Hitler instead, for the sake of appeasing him. British Prime Minister Neville Chamberlain, with the blessings of French leaders, offered Hitler the Sudetenland—the western section of Czechoslovakia that was occupied mostly by Germans. In return Chamberlain received a written assurance that Germany would never invade Great Britain. It was a promise Hitler would later break, but it allowed Europe to sleep easier for a while.

With enemy nations too weak to interfere, ordinary German citizens willing to support Hitler's regime, and Hitler's political power growing stronger and broader every day, Hitler at last found himself ready to activate one of his most cherished plans—the total and final purification of Germany.

Two

The Night of Broken Glass

KRISTALLNACHT BEGAN WITH WHAT SEEMS like a relatively minor incident. It is testament to the belief that one person, acting on his own in a moment of wild emotion, can change the world.

Anger had been brewing inside Herschel Grynszpan for as long as he could remember; there had never been a time when he didn't find life difficult or unpleasant. He was born into poverty on March 28, 1921, the youngest of eight children, only three of whom survived into adulthood. His parents, Sendel and Rivka Grynszpan, were Jews who had emigrated from Poland to Germany in 1911 to escape persecution.

In 1936, with Hitler's anti-Jewish movement gathering steam, he was offered the chance to move to Paris to live with an uncle. The uncle was kind and generous, giving Herschel pocket money and helping him find a job. Herschel liked Paris and decided to remain there. But because he was considered a foreigner, he never received full French citizenship, and in August 1938 he was ordered to leave the country. He became so frustrated and desperate that he considered committing suicide.

Kristallnacht

When he began hearing regular reports of Jews being driven out of Germany by the Nazis, he feared for the safety of his family. Repeated attempts to contact them proved fruitless. Then, on November 3, 1938, he received a message from his sister, Bertie. Her words were chilling:

> You have undoubtedly heard of our great misfortune. I will give you a description of what happened: On Thursday night there were rumors circulating that all Polish Jews of a certain city had been expelled. However, we refused to believe them. On Thursday night at 9:00 PM, a Schupo [police officer] came to our house and told us we had to go to police headquarters with our passports. We went just as we were, all together, to the police headquarters, accompanied by the Schupo. There we found almost our entire neighborhood already assembled. A police wagon then took us at once to the Rathaus [town hall]. Everyone was taken there. We had not yet been told what it was about, but we quickly realized that it was the end for us. An expulsion order was thrust into our hands. We had to leave Germany before October 29 (Saturday). We were not allowed to return to our homes. I begged to be allowed to return home to get at least a few essential things. So I left with a Schupo accompanying me and I packed a valise with the most necessary clothes. That is all I could save. We don't have a cent.

They made it to the Polish-German border but could not get permission to cross. Once again life was dealing the Grynszpan family a vicious blow. Their situation was dire, and Herschel was powerless to help. His anger reached a boiling point and, a few days later, he snapped.

On the morning of November 7 Herschel went to a Paris hotel, had breakfast, showered and dressed, and wrote a brief farewell message to his aunt and uncle on the back of a photograph of himself. Then he left the hotel and walked to a local shop to purchase a gun. When the owner asked what he needed it for, he said he was from out of town and carrying large sums of cash on behalf of a business his father owned. He was given the gun, which he took to a nearby restaurant. In the bathroom he loaded it with bullets, then placed it in the pocket of his coat. Then he traveled to the German embassy, where he gained entrance with the explanation that he had important documents to deliver. He was politely ushered into the office of Ernst vom Rath, an embassy employee.

Vom Rath offered Grynszpan a chair and said, "Did you have an important document to give me?" Grynszpan rose, pulled the gun from his pocket, and replied, "You are a filthy boche [rascal], and here, in the name of 12,000 persecuted Jews, is your document." He then fired five shots into vom Rath at point-blank range.

In spite of the severity of his wounds vom Rath managed to get to the door and call for help. Grynszpan made no attempt to escape. He was promptly captured and taken into custody. Vom Rath, meanwhile, was rushed to a nearby hospital. Despite receiving medical attention swiftly, he died two days after the attack. Before his passing, however, he reported that Grynszpan had shot him as an act of vengeance against the Nazis' treatment of the Jews.

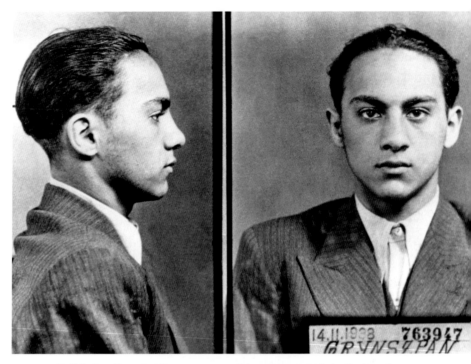

Polish Jew Herschel Grynszpan was taken into custody by Paris police on November 7, 1938, after shooting German embassy employee Ernst vom Rath.

Upon hearing of the incident, Adolf Hitler became outraged. He ordered a highly publicized state funeral for vom Rath, treating him as a national hero and, more important, as a martyr for the Nazi cause. Meanwhile, Nazi-run newspapers ran blaring headlines condemning the murder and stories that it was proof of the ongoing Jewish effort to undermine Nazi leadership and destroy Germany. Hitler also ordered that all Jewish-run newspapers—there were still a few, acting as a kind of communication outlet for Jewish leaders—immediately cease publication and that Jewish children no longer be permitted to attend state schools. Grynszpan's act of rage, it seemed, had served only to increase Hitler's own hatred for the Jewish people.

Convenient Excuse

Hitler had been hoping to make a violent and definitive move against the remaining Jews in Germany for a while. He realized that his goal of creating a Fatherland that was *Judenfrei*—literally, "free of Jews"—would require aggressive action beyond the passage of laws. Grynszpan's murder of vom Rath gave him the perfect excuse to take this step.

On the evening of November 8, with vom Rath still in the hospital and clinging to life, the first attacks began. In the provinces of Hesse and Magdeburg-Anhalt Jews were randomly beaten, their homes and businesses looted, and their synagogues set on fire. The next day, as the Nazi media continued spreading the word and more attacks on Jews broke out across the nation, vom Rath succumbed to his wounds. This gave the Nazi leadership the justification they needed to increase the violence.

Word went out to Nazi officials that they should engage in spontaneous actions against Jewish citizens in every sector of the country. The Storm Troopers were encouraged to have what was later termed a "terroristic fling." Law-enforcement entities—from ordinary police to Hitler's Gestapo—were ordered to do nothing to stop the carnage. Kristallnacht was under way.

Pogrom

The word pogrom comes from the Russian *norpom* (deviation), and its literal meaning is "to wreak havoc; to demolish violently." Although it has been applied to many events

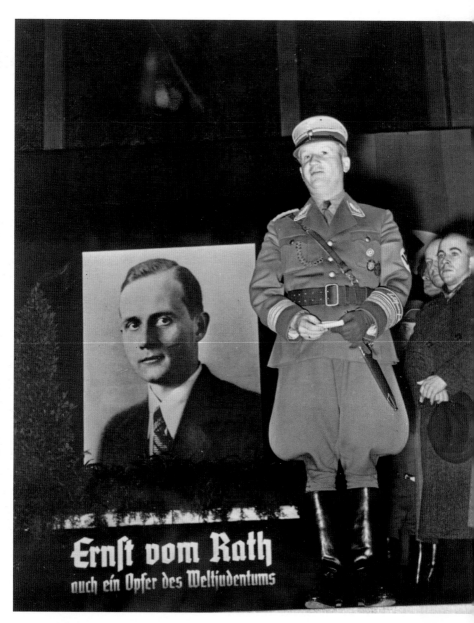

A Nazi propaganda leader speaks at the 1938 opening of the anti-Semitic exhibition called "The Eternal Jew" in Berlin. The poster depicts Ernst vom Rath and reads "Another victim of international Jewry."

By Any Other Name

The English translation of the word Kristallnacht is "crystal night." Its literal meaning is "night of the broken glass," in reference to the thousands of windows that were smashed. However, several other names for the event have been used through the years. The prefix *Reich-* (Reichkristallnacht) has been added on occasion to underscore that the violence was spearheaded by members of Hitler's Third Reich and therefore imply the state sponsorship of the event. Also used is Pogromnacht, which means "night of havoc and destruction." Another variation denotes the month in which it took place—Novemberpogrome ("November night of havoc and destruction"). It should also be noted that the "night of broken glass" is not to be confused with another swift and violent Nazi purge—the "night of the long knives" (Nacht der langen Messer). This was a series of political executions of opponents of the Nazi Party that was carried out from June 30 to July 2, 1934.

throughout history, it is most commonly associated with the blaze of terror and destruction wrought by the Nazis upon Jews and their institutions from November 9 to 10, 1938.

In Munich, the capital of Bavaria (one of Germany's largest states), the first call to the local fire department was made just before midnight, November 9. A display in a textile shop had been smashed and its contents set ablaze. Mere minutes later, on November 10, the first of several synagogue fires was reported. One was burning next to a Jewish schoolhouse. When firemen tried to quell the flames to keep the schoolhouse intact, police not only forced them to stop but poured gasoline on the blaze so it would spread faster. As Jewish homes and businesses caught fire, non-Jewish citizens rushed to help but were blocked by police. At around two o'clock Joseph Goebbels, Hitler's propaganda minister (in charge of Nazi media), received word of the first Jewish death in Munich. There would be nearly twenty deaths in Bavaria before it was all over, about half of them suicides — the rest were murders.

In Berlin, the German capital, the attacks were made with machinelike efficiency. Police cordoned off specific sections of the city (those with the heaviest Jewish influence), then shut down power and gas lines so as to minimize the possibility of accidents. Once these preparations were finalized, Storm Troopers entered and went to work. A family who lived in one of the Berlin synagogues was burned to death, and two Jews who had been chased by a Nazi mob were forced to jump from high windows, killing themselves in the process. A shop that became the focus of a particularly vigorous attack bore the name "Israel's." It was a large

Onlookers view a smashed Jewish shop window in Berlin following the pogrom on the night of November 9, 1938.

department store catering mostly to middle-class citizens, and it had enjoyed a prosperous run since the early 1800s. Around 2:00 PM, members of Hitler's SS entered and removed all Jewish employees. Then the store was summarily looted and destroyed. Unwanted products were thrown through windows, scattering glass on the street. Police did surround the property, but only to make sure ordinary citizens didn't get too close to the rubble and injure themselves. In Jewish homes the SS roundups continued. They focused primarily on the wealthier areas because they were better for looting. Men were beaten and women raped. Then they were arrested and removed, rarely being permitted to take even a single bag of necessities with them—a luxury that the Nazis had usually permitted in the past.

In Bremen orders came down from Joseph Goebbels that SA men were to carry out their attacks against Jews without wearing their uniforms. Unfortunately, someone in the chain of communication got this wrong, and many SA did wear their uniforms. The purpose of Goebbels's order was, incredibly, to make it appear as though the attacks were spontaneous actions by ordinary citizens rather than the product of direct orders on the part of Nazi leadership.

It turned out to be a minor point in the end. Houses and businesses in Bremen were cleaned out and then destroyed, and synagogues burned as firefighters stood by for the sole purpose of making sure the blazes didn't spread to non-Jewish properties. After some official discussion, the wording of anti-Jewish signs was agreed upon, and they were posted throughout the city. One approved slogan read "Death to International Jewry." Storm Troopers even ransacked a Jewish cemetery, defacing and smashing headstones. In one home an elderly Jewish man resisted arrest and was promptly shot.

In the neighboring village of Lesum, Nazi officials, astonished by what was happening elsewhere in the country, consulted with party leaders to make sure their orders were

This Berlin synagogue was destroyed by a blaze set by the Nazi SS.

clear. They were told that yes, in retribution for Grynszpan's murder of vom Rath, the "Jewish problem" was going to be solved that night. Lesum's officials then went to the homes of local Jewish residents and murdered them in their beds.

In Leipzig, a city in the eastern German state of Saxony, the Nazi Party held a most bizarre ritual on the night of November 9, in preparation for their own pogrom.

Kristallnacht

In celebration of Adolf Hitler's Beer Hall Putsch—the attempted overthrow of the German government by Hitler and a group of his early followers on the same date fifteen years earlier—exhumed remains of Hitler's comrades from the failed coup were displayed in splendor in a city square, with draped banners, smoking urns, flaming torches, and columns of marching soldiers. Many in the crowd found it macabre and overdramatic, but the Nazis were moved by it to heights of almost intoxicated inspiration.

Following this bizarre ceremony, SA and SS moved swiftly and eagerly to carry out their secret orders to terrorize all Jews in the Leipzig area. More windows were smashed, and more homes and businesses were burned. Treasured possessions flew from high windows to the streets below—often followed by Jewish citizens who'd been foolish enough to resist their tormentors. Synagogues were firebombed and allowed to burn down to their foundations, while Jews— including children—were beaten mercilessly, then arrested and hauled away, never to be seen again.

In the city of Cologne (Köln), located near Germany's western border, police were given an order to do more than simply stand aside; they were told to take part in the attacks. They had to round up recruits to help with the looting, pillaging, and abuse of Jewish citizens. They also had to make sure the willing participants were properly supplied (e.g., they should not run low on axes, ladders, bricks and stones, and gasoline to keep the fires burning). They also had to help distinguish Jewish businesses from non-Jewish businesses and do the same for apartments and houses. In a moment of dark comedy one policeman

In Linz, Jewish women were put on display as their hair was shaved off in public. They were forced to wear a sign that read, "I have been ostracized from the national community."

tried to stop a Nazi member from looting a Jewish store that had already been destroyed because of a government order that valuables in a damaged building be left intact or removed only for preservation purposes, and that the state maintain control of them. He was summarily arrested and punished. More than four hundred Jews were arrested in Cologne that night, all under the guise that they were being held for their own protection. Many of those who wished to leave the city were told they could have the necessary paperwork—for prices so high, they were left almost penniless. In one instance a Jewish man was forced to sell his business to a Nazi competitor for less than 1/100th of its true value, then was fined that amount by a Nazi judge for committing crimes against the German government.

In and around Frankfurt, located in central Germany in the state of Hesse, Jews were rounded up and taken by the truckload to a large public hall. Crowds had formed outside and shouted insults, threw stones, and spit on the incoming prisoners. The Jews were then robbed of all valuables and forced to sit huddled together without food or water for days. For amusement Nazi officials forced them to do exercises until they collapsed from exhaustion—or, in the case of one elderly man, death. Another was dragged around by his beard. In the town itself mobs moved in packs of five to ten, led by SA or SS officers, going from property to property with gruesome efficiency, making certain not to touch homes or businesses that belonged to Nazis, other non-Jewish Germans, or (to their disappointment) Jews of foreign citizenry. They had been ordered by Nazi leadership to forgo attacks on foreign Jews so as to avoid possible diplomatic incidents.

In Würzburg one Jewish businessman suffered a stroke while sitting in a local jail cell. The Nazis took their time

Increasing the Indignity

As if simply destroying their homes, businesses, and synagogues wasn't sufficient, many participants in Kristallnacht further humiliated Jews by forcing them to engage in ridiculous acts, often for the sake of Nazi amusement. In one instance a rabbi was made to stand at the front of his synagogue and recite from Hitler's *Mein Kampf* while members of his congregation listened. He remembered, "I was summoned from the dais to read a passage from *Mein Kampf*. I began softly, but the SS troops behind me grew irritated and struck me on the back of my neck. Those who read afterwards received the same treatment." In another instance two young Jewish boys had to paint anti-Semitic slurs on the windows of a business their father owned. A young woman who worked as an opera singer was made to stand on a table in her apartment and recite Nazi marching songs while being held at gunpoint. And an elderly Jewish woman was required to gather up all the Torah scrolls in her home and toss them into a nearby river.

getting him to a hospital, where he died the next day. In the same town, three Jewish women committed suicide after their husbands were taken by SS officers—one by poison, another by drowning, and the third by hanging. Würzburg was also the town in which a board game could be purchased—suitable for adults and children alike—called "Jews Out!"

In Elbing a Jewish man who had lost his vision while fighting in World War I took his thirteen-year-old son to their local synagogue in the hope of rescuing the boy's prayer book, ceremonial clothing, and other items. When they reached the synagogue, it was too late—everything of value had been consumed by the blaze, and the building was almost gone. There was, however, a crowd surrounding the property, cheering.

In Vienna a Jewish man's shop was looted by his competitors, then destroyed by SA members. Once the destruction was complete, the owner was forced to clean up the mess. When that was finished, the store was confiscated by the Nazis—but the man still had to pay taxes on it. Penniless, he went out one night to sell his wedding band in order to raise the money—and was arrested by SS officers. Elsewhere in the city, as news of vom Rath's death spread, ordinary citizens turned viciously on Jews right in the streets, in broad daylight. Nazi officials, naturally, made no effort to stop them—many, in fact, were seen walking about, offering encouragement. Much of the contents of a school for rabbis was piled in the street outside and turned into a huge bonfire. One Jewish eyewitness to the Viennese carnage, just fourteen years old at the time, remembered,

The next day I met a friend and we went
up to the synagogue. We found it trashed
and devastated. . . . We were interrupted by
two men, wearing the obligatory jackboots,
swastika armband and Tyrolean hats who
had come to relish the destruction. . . . We
scurried down the stairs and sadly departed
from the synagogue we had frequently
attended with our parents.

In Aachen Nazis smashed up a Jewish-owned café while non-Jewish citizens stole food and drinks, then ate and drank as they watched from the glass-littered sidewalk. And in Hamburg a young Jewish woman emerged from a long train ride and raced to her parents' house. She found the house empty and soon learned that they had been taken away. She would never see them again.

Final Tally

Although history books usually record that the Kristallnacht pogrom lasted from November 9 to 10, lingering violence continued for several days in some areas. When it finally ended, the damage was horrifying—almost 100 Jews murdered and more than 30,000 arrested; many were sent to detention camps and held there for weeks and months. Nearly all the synagogues in Germany and Austria were burned to the ground, along with their precious, often irreplaceable contents. Thousands more Jewish homes and businesses were looted and destroyed or confiscated by Nazi Party members. All remaining Jews, who were forbidden by

Kristallnacht

Nazi law to make insurance claims, were ordered to pay for the damage—and if they didn't have the money (which most didn't), they were forced to give up a percentage of their remaining property.

Despite the destruction, Kristallnacht did not mark the end of suffering for Jews in Hitler's Germany. In many ways it was just the beginning.

Three
Reaction

NOT ALL GERMANS WHO STOOD BY and did nothing did so because they quietly approved of the pogrom. The general reaction to Kristallnacht among non-Jewish German citizens was one of horror and outrage, but most simply could not turn their sentiments into actions. What held them back from formal protest was the same basic fear the Nazis had cultivated since Hitler's ascension to power—that those who dared intervene would suffer the same fate as the Jews themselves. Along with delivering a massive blow to the Jewish presence in the growing German empire, the Nazis sent a chilling message to the rest of the population—do as you are expected, or there will be consequences. Many years later Hans Bernd Gisevius, a Nazi intelligence official, wrote, "the cowed middle class stared at the Nazi monster like a rabbit at a snake. A general psychosis had been created . . . and this effect was valuable to the Nazis." Ordinary German citizens who had their own homes, professions to which they had devoted their adult lives, and relatives they cared for were hesitant to take risks.

A shopkeeper in the northern town of Beckum reported, "I remember the Reichkristallnacht well. . . . I heard, over and over again, in the street, walking, running, shouting, windows being broken. [The SS] had driven the Jews out into the street. They had beaten them up so badly they needed to go into hospital. . . . Most people stayed in their homes. They were just glad not to have been involved." Another Beckum resident recalled, "My father was crying and wanted to stop them, but my mother held him back. He recognized the danger and closed the window."

Word also spread that members of the SS, disguised in ordinary clothing, walked among crowds during and after Kristallnacht in the hope of overhearing dissenting comments. Those who were foolish enough to voice such opinions might be followed to their homes, beaten, and then arrested.

In spite of these enormous risks some citizens did summon the courage to take a stand. Their acts were often passive, as evidenced by the flood of angry, usually anonymous letters received by foreign embassies and media outlets from ordinary German citizens. In a similar spirit many people gave money and basic necessities to Jewish families by anonymously leaving packages in their mailboxes, doorways, and foyers.

Others reacted in a more overt fashion. Some offered temporary hiding places for fleeing Jews to escape arrest and detention until they could be moved out of the country. Another tactic was to transfer ownership of Jewish-owned goods to non-Jewish friends so the Nazis wouldn't confiscate them. It wasn't unusual for ownership of everything from jewelry to cars to apartment buildings to be suddenly transferred. In Berlin on the day after the violence, a woman who owned an apartment building lied to a pair of SS officers about the whereabouts of two of her Jewish tenants so they would give up their hunt. If she had been caught, she could have been punished by imprisonment or even death.

The truly bold chose to speak out publicly, even with the knowledge that the consequences would be dire. Lutheran pastor Julius von Jan said bitterly to his congregation, "Houses of worship, sacred to others, have been burned down with impunity. . . . Our nation's infamy is bound to bring about divine punishment." For his courageous speech von Jan was shortly thereafter attacked by a Nazi squad, beaten into unconsciousness, and thrown in jail. His house was also destroyed.

There were even members of the Nazi Party who took offense to Kristallnacht. Several of the SA and SS who had not been directly involved in the violence resigned their positions. Some said they still held fervent anti-Semitic beliefs but were against manifesting them in such violent fashion. Similarly, there were German citizens who considered themselves casual followers of the Nazi ideology who also denounced the party. A few even said they were ashamed to be German.

There were those outside the Nazi Party who applauded Kristallnacht. Historian Ian Kershaw, who wrote several books about Hitler and the Nazi regime, noted, "Ordinary citizens . . . followed the Party's lead in many places and joined in the destruction and looting of Jewish property. Schoolchildren and adolescents were frequently ready the next day to add

A Puzzling Contrast

In spite of the Nazis' dark history of cruelty against Jews, there remains a peculiar incongruity in the persona of the high-ranking Nazi official Hermann Göring. While Göring faithfully served Adolf Hitler's anti-Semitic agenda—and was rewarded for his loyalty in many ways, including his appointment both as Hitler's eventual successor as the leader of the Third Reich as well as commander of Hitler's Luftwaffe (air force)—there is strong evidence that he also protected certain Jews to whom he had taken a liking. Those under his military command who were particularly good soldiers but had Jewish heritage, for example, were spared persecution through the creation of false birth certificates. He also saved a pair of Jewish couples from a concentration camp because they had aided him after he sustained wounds during the Beer Hall Putsch in 1923. The four Jews were, on Göring's orders, taken safely out of

Germany. Regardless of these flashes of decency, Göring was sentenced to death during the Nuremberg War Trials (see page 92) following World War II for his complicity with the Nazi Party.

This illustration from a children's book issued by the anti-Semitic German weekly *Der Sturmer* depicts Aryan children celebrating the removal of a Jewish teacher and students from their German school.

their taunts, jibes, and insults to Jews being rounded up by the police." In Berlin, while one of the synagogues was burning, a woman was overheard to say, "That's the right way to do it—it's a pity there aren't any more Jews inside."

Around the World

Some European nations expressed their support of Kristall-nacht. Leaders in Italy, Romania, and Hungary—all dictators—put their stamp of approval on the pogrom, plus they gave their support for a few radically nationalistic and anti-Semitic groups in Poland. (Italy, Romania, and Hungary would later become allies of Hitler at the start of World War II.)

In religious circles there were only faint and individual cries of protest. Most Protestants and Catholics alike, both within Germany and beyond its borders, were noticeably passive about the pogrom or approved of it. Many German Christians were loyal to Hitler—they were abundant within Nazi ranks—and found joy not only in attacking Jews for political and economic reasons but also for religious ones.

A few European nations regarded Kristallnacht in a calculatedly mild fashion. Many were direct neighbors of Germany that did not wish to spoil relations with Hitler even though they disagreed with his actions. The French, for example, could not afford to ignore the fact that Hitler's military was within easy striking distance—not to mention that many French citizens carried their own distaste for Jews. In Switzerland the official response to the pogrom was tepid at best—there was also a fair amount of anti-Semitism among the Swiss at the time, so they had little interest in encouraging the mass emigration of refugees. Several other European nations also took this approach, minimizing the blame for Kristallnacht on the Nazis so as not to send a sympathetic message to fleeing Jews. Similarly, Russia, located east of

Germany on the other side of Poland, didn't even mention Kristallnacht in its state-run newspaper, *Pravda*, until nearly a week after it took place. The newspaper did speak strongly against the brutality and foolishness of Hitler's regime, but this was mostly bluster; while Joseph Stalin's government was happy to scold the Nazis for their cruelty, it had no intention of offering German Jews immigration opportunities or any other form of relief.

One European nation did take a firm stance against the horrors of Kristallnacht and wasn't afraid to say so—Great Britain. Screaming headlines from every major newspaper attacked Hitler, and political and religious leaders made speeches railing against Nazi savagery while warning that it was a dark omen of troubling times ahead. England apparently had no fear of compromising its relationship with Hitler's government, in spite of its close proximity to Germany and the fact that Hitler's military was growing ever more powerful.

The United States stood alongside England in its condemnation. Newspapers across the nation fired away at Hitler and the Nazis, as noted figures on every stage spoke out. *The New York Times* stated, "Jews Are Beaten, Furniture and Goods Flung From Homes and Shops—15,000 Are Jailed During Day—20 Are Suicides." Former president Herbert Hoover took aim at those responsible by saying, "These men are building their own condemnation by mankind for centuries to come. . . . It is still my belief that the German people, if they could express themselves, would not approve these acts against the Jews." And Thomas E. Dewey, a New York prosecutor who would one day run for the presidency as the Republican challenger to

Harry S. Truman, wrote, "Not since the days of medieval barbarism has the world been forced to look upon a spectacle such as this." Some tried to figure out the Nazis' motivation. An editorial in *The New York Times* suggested that part of Hitler's motivation for targeting Jews was financial—to "make a profit for itself out of legalized loot," while the *Baltimore Sun* similarly labeled it a "money collecting enterprise." Meanwhile, demonstrations were taking place all across the United States, with some protesters

New York's garment and fur workers stage a protest in November 1938 denouncing the treatment of Jews in Germany.

The Kindertransport

In early December 1938 a train carrying more than two hundred refugee children pulled into the British station in Harwich. It was the first of what would be many such journeys to become known as the Kindertransport (and those on board known as Kinder). Great Britain had agreed to take as many children as possible following Kristallnacht, with special priority given to orphans, children with only one parent, those who had already lost parents to the concentration camps, or those old enough to be considered for arrest themselves. Sadly, many of the parents of the Kinder would not survive the war, leaving the children homeless and with bleak prospects. Nevertheless, in the nine months that the Kindertransport operated, more than 10,000 youngsters were saved from Nazi savagery.

going so far as burning Nazi flags and effigies of Hitler and his henchmen. Even in Canada, normally placid and neutral concerning international affairs in which it had no direct role, there were cries of anger and formal protests.

Any Port in a Storm

Long before Kristallnacht German Jews had received the clear message that Hitler and his Nazi government wanted them out of the country. Between the random acts of violence and the countless laws enacted to diminish their standing in society, it would be hard to imagine anyone thinking otherwise. Nevertheless, many had lived in Germany all their lives, had extensive ancestral roots there, and had come to love their homeland and therefore didn't want to leave. After Kristallnacht, however, even the most deeply rooted Jews realized that emigration was the only sensible option.

As soon as the pogrom ended, thousands fled for the borders, hoping to cross into Belgium, France, Switzerland, or, ironically, Poland—a nation that had been forced by neighboring Russia to drive thousands of Jews into Germany years before during several ethnic purges of its own. Others applied for entry visas to foreign lands that could be reached by train or boat.

The problem was that most countries weren't prepared for immigration on such a massive scale. Italy, to no one's surprise, flatly denied entry to all refugees. Italian leader Benito Mussolini ran his nation in the same dictatorial fashion as Hitler and was, in fact, one of Hitler's closest friends and allies. Russia, too, had made it clear that it

Jewish refugees from Germany wait to escape to bordering countries.

was unwilling to open its doors. It did it in a fairly under-handed fashion—by first saying it would permit a modest number of immigrants, but only under certain terms and conditions that, as it turned out, were impossible for any German Jew to meet.

In South America several nations were more polite and diplomatic in their refusal. Brazil, Argentina, Paraguay, Uruguay, and Chile, for example, claimed they would've been happy to accommodate refugees under ordinary circumstances, but they already had immigration problems to deal with. In South Africa the explanation was that Jews were likely unable to blend into their society. Many governments, it seemed, had an excuse ready.

A group called the Intergovernmental Committee for Refugees had been formed in the summer of 1938 to help German Jews resettle in other parts of the world. It was run mostly by representatives from Great Britain and the United States, but it also had input from other European nations, plus a few in South America. After Kristallnacht the committee accelerated its efforts, hoping to find one or two large areas that Jews could, in essence, call their own. Madagascar, a massive French-governed island off the southeastern coast of Africa, was one possibility. It had a wealth of natural resources and a fairly pleasant climate. But there were questions over what would become of the existing Madagascar natives, how many Jews would be allowed to settle there, and whether any forthcoming wars with Germany would extend into the region due to the sudden Jewish presence. France also insisted that other nations would have to pitch in and take their share of refugees as well—if not, then none would be welcome in Madagascar. The idea was eventually dropped. Another suggestion was the Portuguese colony of Angola, but Portugal's dictator immediately rejected this, since he had about as much sympathy for Jewish suffering as

Hitler did. Areas of Venezuela and the Philippines were also discussed, but natives of both nations vehemently opposed the notion.

There were a few countries and governments that made a sincere effort to do what they could. Holland took in tens of thousands of Jews, focusing on the immigrants' well-being first and worrying about the logistical problems their arrival caused later. Since Hitler's rise to power in 1933, Holland had taken more than 25,000 immigrants, most of whom had some Jewish ancestry. After Kristallnacht that number skyrocketed to more than 1,000 *per week*. Belgium also took a few thousand immigrants, as did the South American nation of Honduras—a poor nation aware that immigration would only help its situation. Canada had already taken more than 6,000 refugees since Hitler took power, and Czechoslovakia had accepted more than four times that many. Australia, which had previously refused to accept any Jewish immigrants, granted entry to more than 5,000 in the year following the pogrom. And France, in spite of its native anti-Semitism and grumbling about potential refugee problems, ended up permitting many thousands of Jews to cross its borders. Even if the understanding was that the Jews would only be allowed to remain there temporarily, at least the French provided a safe haven.

The nation that ended up doing the most for fleeing German Jews was Great Britain. It was perhaps the most powerful empire in the world at the time, with influence all over the globe. One area the empire had governed since the end of World War I was the geographic region known as

Palestine, which lay between the Mediterranean Sea and the Jordan River and would eventually become the State of Israel. Long before Kristallnacht the British had been allowing Jews to settle in Palestine by the thousands. After Kristallnacht they considered inviting many thousands more. The main problem was that the Arabs who already lived in Palestine could not seem to forge a friendly and

A group of Jewish children are led to London's Victoria Railway Station on their way to Palestine.

symbiotic relationship with the immigrant Jews. In fact, each group's intense dislike of the other led to seemingly endless skirmishes that often turned bloody and resulted in many deaths on both sides. It was particularly disappointing to British leaders, who saw the potential for Palestine to become the home for masses of German Jews. But the Arab world, loyal to its Palestinian brothers, would not hear of it, and Britain wanted to maintain its diplomatic friendships with other Arab countries. In the end the British brought hundreds of thousands of Jewish refugees into their own land, some until they could be resettled elsewhere, some permanently.

In the United States President Roosevelt tried desperately to help Germany's Jews, but he faced an uphill battle on every front. First, the rate at which the U.S. government was accepting immigrants had dropped sharply since the Great Depression. Most political leaders, not to mention the millions of American citizens who were suffering, felt that the economy simply could not support the weight of a massive influx of foreigners. Second, although Roosevelt was sympathetic to the plight of the German Jews, he was shackled by a Republican-ruled Congress that was already angry about his New Deal policies, which favored the poor and underprivileged over the wealthy. Roosevelt and his supporters did manage to arrange for the immigration of a few thousand Jews, but that didn't put much of a dent in the problem—there were still hundreds of thousands in Germany searching desperately for an exit.

Carefully surveying the situation from all angles, Hitler could not have been more delighted. There was outcry and protest from every corner of the earth, and nations were assailing him with a variety of threats. Ultimately, however, none made a move to stop him. Emboldened by the relatively passive response to Kristallnacht by the other nations of the world, he came up with a plan to deal with the Jewish problem that became known as the Final Solution.

Four
A Nightmare Beyond Measure

INCREDIBLE AS IT MAY SEEM, Nazi leadership made a concerted effort, with Joseph Goebbels at the helm, to strike back against the rest of the world where media coverage of Kristallnacht was concerned. Goebbels began by banning from Germany every major foreign newspaper that negatively reported on the pogrom. Then he coordinated a public relations counteroffensive by having Nazi-run papers publish blistering editorials about similar examples of racial mistreatment in other nations. He accused countries such as the United States and Great Britain of being run by hypocrites because they railed against Nazi attitudes toward Jews while harboring their own set of prejudices against various ethnic groups (including Jews).

Meanwhile, the Nazi high command made sure to delay vom Rath's burial, eking every ounce of publicity and drama out of it. His body was placed in a splendid coffin and set on a slow-moving train to the western town of Düsseldorf, where his family lived. There the coffin was displayed in a large hall, draped with a Nazi flag and surrounded by representatives from the SS, SA, Hitler Youth, and other state organizations.

As Hitler's propaganda chief, Joseph Goebbels broadcast Nazi philosophy through all media outlets.

Hundreds of mourners filed past, many barely aware of who vom Rath even was. Then Hitler arrived, ever the compassionate leader, and took a seat between the victim's parents. He sat humbly and quietly during the service, then spoke to the vom Raths before departing. The body was moved by carriage through the streets before being interred in a family vault at the local cemetery. The service was reported on throughout the country with the intention of soliciting understanding for the people's anger toward Jews.

The Price of Inaction

Around the world, once the initial shock had faded and Hitler realized he would pay no substantial price for Kristallnacht, savagery toward the remaining Jewish population began anew. During this wave of violence, however, the Nazis no longer made a half-hearted effort to hide their actions. Jews were not permitted simply to walk through certain areas of their own towns and villages. They couldn't visit public parks or swimming pools or museums, lest they pay a steep fine or serve time in prison. In a conversation with other Nazi leaders Joseph Goebbels said,

> There are some Jews who don't look
> Jewish who plonk themselves down beside
> German mothers and their children and try
> telling them all sorts of things. I think this
> is a definite danger and we must therefore
> reserve special parks for Jews—not the
> beautiful ones, naturally—and specify which
> benches they shall be allowed to use.

Jewish physicians could no longer treat anyone who wasn't also Jewish. All remaining Jewish businesses were to be transferred to non-Jewish owners. Veterans of the German or Austrian military who were Jewish were forbidden to wear their uniforms in spite of the fact that they had risked their lives for their countries. Jews were also relieved of all driving privileges and in fact were no longer allowed to even own motorized vehicles. And the few remaining Jewish children who attended school in Germany or Austria were permanently expelled.

Elderly Berlin citizens sit on a park bench marked "Not for Jews."

The purpose of these manifold cruelties was, of course, to encourage all Jews still in the country to leave as quickly as possible. Goebbels, again driven by the arrogance that comes from having no fear of reprisal, said in a speech less than two weeks after Kristallnacht, "We would like the whole world to become so friendly to the Jews that it would absorb all [of ours]!"

Foreign governments still didn't make an effort to stop Hitler and his Nazi Party. The majority, it seemed, were waiting for the three leading powers—the United States, Britain, and France—to do something first. (The other major power at the time, Russia, clearly had little interest in taking action against Germany—although this would change in time.) U.S. president Franklin Roosevelt, who felt a degree of sympathy for German Jews, was hamstrung by the fact that his citizens were disinterested in getting involved in any conflict that didn't directly affect the United States. They felt that Hitler was Europe's problem.

Leaders in Great Britain and France didn't take action because they were still hoping to create more stable relations with Hitler's government. In late September 1938, mere weeks before Kristallnacht, British and French leaders had handed Hitler the Sudetenland—the western section of Czechoslovakia that was occupied largely by people of German heritage—in a pact called the Munich Agreement. Hitler had earlier threatened to invade Czechoslovakia, so this was their idea of a compromise. In return Hitler promised not to overrun any other parts of Europe. After feeling the devastating effects of World War I and the Great Depression, the last thing the leaders of Britain and France wanted was another military conflict—and Hitler knew this. So before

Constructive Engagement versus Appeasement

It may seem to some that the strategy of trying to appease Hitler by giving him bits and pieces of what he wanted was foolish. Looking back on it now, England, France, and others may have seemed overly idealistic for adopting such an approach. At the time, however, this was considered a normal part of diplomatic policy. Known as constructive engagement, this policy was used to give rogue nations as many chances as possible to change their ways. It formed the basis of many solid relationships between nations around the world, and it usually worked. Constructive engagement was a better strategy than either ignoring rogue nations or engaging them in military exchanges. Hitler's European neighbors were hoping to contain him rather than drag the continent into another conflict, and they should be commended for attempting to keep the situation civilized. It was Hitler who ultimately cast aside all promises made and sparked the beginnings of World War II, which led to the death of millions.

the brutality of Kristallnacht, Hitler enjoyed the benefits of a policy of appeasement. Also, Nazi leaders made it clear, both publicly and through private diplomatic channels, that any retaliation against them for Kristallnacht would result in further action against the Jews under their governance—a population that now included those in Germany, Austria, and the Sudetenland.

As if all of this wasn't enough, Hitler gave a speech in January 1939 in which he stressed his desire to build productive relations with other nations while wishing to achieve "the annihilation of the Jewish race throughout Europe."

The Concentration Camps

A concentration camp is a secured area that holds great numbers of noncombatant prisoners during a war or similar conflict. These prisoners are usually incarcerated for political reasons, such as being suspected of playing some role in aiding an enemy nation or having some connection to that nation (like being an immigrant). It is not uncommon for such prisoners to be incarcerated without having first been legally tried; they are simply captured and sent off. Nevertheless, under ideal conditions, they are treated humanely through the provision of sufficient food, shelter, and clothing; the freedom to communicate with relatives abroad; and interaction with other inmates to facilitate some sense of community during their stay.

The Nazis arrested thousands of people, Jews among them, during the 1930s and shipped them off to concentration camps. Even before Hitler's rise to power in 1933, secret camps were being used throughout Germany to hold anyone perceived as a threat to the Nazi Party or people the party leaders deemed undesirable. This included political opponents, those who sympathized with Jews, gypsies, convicted criminals, vagrants, homosexuals, the elderly, and even the mentally and physically challenged.

The Nazis tried to paint a rosy picture of life in their camps. Propaganda films were produced showing happy, well-fed people in clean clothes living in respectable surroundings. They may have been prisoners in the technical sense, these films implied, but they were treated with all due decency. Relatives would receive postcards from camp inmates assuring them everything was all right, that their needs were being attended to, and so on.

In reality, Nazi concentration camps were home to unspeakable hardship and brutality. By the time Kristallnacht took place, many inmates were being utilized as forced laborers in various Nazi-run business ventures. They engaged in everything from making weapons and ammunition to car parts and building materials. Very few of the thousands of inmates were paid any wages. Most worked for free, often under the false promise that they would be released after a certain amount of time, and under appalling conditions. They had to endure extremes of both heat and cold, were given very little food, and were severely punished if they didn't produce. Anyone perceived as lazy or otherwise unproductive would be beaten, tortured, and sometimes killed. Those who became injured and could no longer work were routinely put to death.

The great majority of Nazi concentration camps were located in quiet, isolated areas so no one would know about them. As Hitler's armies marched through other parts of Europe and captured more Jews and other "undesirables,"

Prisoners at the Dachau concentration camp were worked like slaves, manufacturing German weapons and ammunition.

more forced-labor camps had to be established. During Hitler's reign Germany's economy swelled to impressive proportions, since so many millions of workers were not being paid.

The concentration camp was one of two types of camps the Nazis established to deal with their enemies. The other was even worse.

Broken Promises

In March 1939 Hitler again broke a promise he'd made; he overran the rest of Czechoslovakia. Again, the British and the French complained but took no action. Encouraged, Hitler then invaded Poland in September 1939. Finally, Great Britain and France abandoned their strategy of constructive engagement and formally declared war on Germany, launching World War II. Undaunted, in April 1940, Hitler sent his forces into both Denmark and Norway, which capitulated almost immediately. By the end of June even France had fallen into the dictator's grip.

The Final Solution

While Hitler was undoubtedly pleased with the ongoing success of his military operations and the rapid expansion of the German empire, the acquisition of so much territory created a new problem for him: more Jewish citizens. Poland, in particular, had the largest Jewish population in all of Europe—more than 3 million. It was difficult enough getting other nations to accept Jewish refugees from Germany after Kristallnacht. What was to be done with the Polish Jews who were now, technically, under his governance?

In 1941 the Nazis began to establish ghettos, demarcated sections of large cities—mostly in Poland—exclusively for Jewish occupation. This would separate them from the rest of society. Hundreds of thousands of Jews were deported from Germany, Austria, and other Nazi-controlled areas. They then had to endure terrible living conditions, including a lack of food and clean water, heat, and medical care. Thousands of elderly and infirm died within weeks of arrival. Those who had the courage to speak up were usually executed

Protecting Their Own

Often overlooked by historians of the Third Reich are the remarkable actions taken by the Turkish government to protect that nation's Jews from Nazi persecution. Turkey, which lay southeast of Germany, had thousands of its citizens living throughout Europe at the time of Hitler's rise to power. When the systematic harassment of Jews began in earnest, Turkish officials committed themselves to protecting their people. They knew that Hitler was hesitant to target foreign Jews—not out of respect but out of concern for stirring up anger in foreign leadership. They used this to their advantage. They instructed their citizens living and traveling abroad to keep their paperwork—which proved their nationality—fully updated at all times. Turkish officials worked almost around the clock to see that those who had allowed their citizenship papers to expire had them swiftly reissued. Sometimes they would even fabricate or altogether invent documents and certificates in order to keep a Turkish Jew out of Nazi hands. It has been estimated that more than 20,000 were saved from the Holocaust as a result of these efforts.

on the spot. Depression was common, leading many ghetto residents to commit suicide.

But the greatest horrors lay beyond the ghettos and concentration camps. By early 1942 Hitler and his top advisors had decided to begin the process of removing all the remaining Jews from Europe through mass genocide, a word not

Jews enter a ghetto established by the Nazis.

even in existence at the time—the Final Solution. They would wait no longer for other nations to provide a safe haven for them, for that would take too long and be too troublesome. Simply eliminating the Jews was a better approach—and, as with the concentration camps, secrecy was of the utmost importance.

Born from the Final Solution came the extermination camps, or death camps. Located mostly in Poland for the sake of convenience (and to keep them in isolated areas in order to retain the needed secrecy), Nazi extermination camps became the setting for some of the most harrowing scenes in human history. Upon their arrival, prisoners were often taunted and beaten by guards. Their heads were shaved, they were given showers, then handed uniforms onto which they were required to sew Jewish stars. Many were left un-fed for days, and any who protested were tortured. A favorite was to hang a prisoner by his arms until his body weight caused the arms to dislocate from their sockets. The pain would become so unbearable that the victim would pass out—at which time a guard would revive him by splashing cold water on his face so he could endure further agony. Another gruesome aspect of camp life was the use of pris-oners for grisly medical experiments.

The camps were surrounded by wire that carried a powerful electrical charge, and many threw themselves onto it to purposely end their lives. Barracks that were built to house fifty people usually held more than a hundred, forcing inmates to sleep huddled together in sweating or freezing masses. Anyone foolish enough to disregard the nightly curfew was shot on sight. Sometimes inmates were attacked by dogs, which the guards would release for the amusement of watching them tear a prisoner to pieces. Since food cost money, the Nazi government simply cut back on the amount given to prisoners. Many went for days without a meal, and millions died from malnourishment. Their bodies weighed a fraction of what they once did and looked like skeletons, the skin stretched tightly across the bones.

The extermination process was carried out with clinical efficiency. Early on prisoners were lined up by the dozens and simply shot by firing squads. But as more arrived, the Nazi leadership realized they had to accelerate the process. They devised gas chambers—large, sealed-off rooms into

Starving prisoners were photographed at a German concentration camp known for carrying out scientific experiments on its inmates.

which hundreds could be crowded and then exposed to poisonous gas. Afterward, camp officers would usually remove gold fillings from the corpses. And if a victim had a particularly attractive tattoo, the skin might be removed, dried, and used to make lampshades or book coverings. One eyewitness remembered,

> Dentists hammered out gold teeth, bridges
> and crowns. In the midst of them stood
> [a Nazi officer]. He was in his element,
> and showing me a large can full of teeth,
> he said: "See for yourself the weight of that
> gold! It's only from yesterday and the day
> before. You can't imagine what we find
> every day—dollars, diamonds, gold. You'll
> see for yourself!"

After the gassings, the bodies were burned in crematoriums specially built for the camps—rows of brick ovens in which hundreds of bodies could be incinerated at a time. If these weren't available, the bodies were dumped into mass graves and covered over. Sometimes for amusement, camp guards would force a prisoner to dig his own grave and carve his name onto a piece of wood—a makeshift headstone—then shoot the prisoner, often in full view of others awaiting the same fate.

The Nightmare Ends

By late 1942 Hitler's forces were beginning to lose momentum in their quest to conquer Europe and beyond. They had waged a successful push into Russia, but then they were

The Fate of Herschel Grynszpan

After being arrested for the shooting of Ernst vom Rath, Herschel Grynszpan was taken to prison in France to await trial. A few weeks later he appeared at a pretrial hearing, at which time his attorney mounted his legal defense. In the end, however, the French government decided to delay the trial for as long as possible, for it was too politically charged. So Grynszpan was returned to prison to wait. When World War II erupted following Hitler's takeover of Poland in September 1939, Grynszpan formally requested to be enlisted in the French military but was denied. He was then moved from prison to prison around the country. Not long after France fell to Germany, in June of 1940, Grynszpan was unofficially released because French prison officials knew the Nazis would come looking for him. Nevertheless, he was captured in early July, taken to Germany for questioning, then imprisoned again in January 1941. He was well cared for—he ate decent food, had clean surroundings, and wasn't required to do much. The Nazis wanted to put him on display in a trial of their own. However, Grynszpan had by this time invented the story that he and vom Rath had been homosexual lovers and that the shooting was the result of a jealous rage. In light of this, Nazi leaders decided against the trial, knowing that the story was Grynszpan's invention but not wanting to risk any damage to vom Rath's (and the Third Reich's) reputation. After this the trail of Herschel Grynszpan all but vanishes. There are scant mentions of him in Nazi documents, a few unsubstantiated sightings, and many rumors. Most believe he was sent to the Sachsenhausen concentration camp at the end of 1942 and died there, but no one knows for sure. His fate remains a mystery to this day.

turned back by the frigid winter of 1942–1943. In July of 1943 Mussolini, the leader of Italy and Hitler's main ally, was arrested, and Italy soon surrendered to the Allied forces. By mid-1944 Germany had lost much of the territory it had gained. In June its forces were driven out of France, and by the end of the year they had abandoned Hungary, Greece, Albania, and Yugoslavia. By April 1945 Russian forces had broken into the German capital of Berlin. On April 30, with Russian forces mere blocks away, Hitler committed suicide by taking a cyanide capsule while simultaneously shooting himself. One of the men who had played a key role in the coordination of Kristallnacht, Joseph Goebbels, followed Hitler's example and took his own life a day later—but not before arranging and overseeing the murder of his six young children. On May 7 German forces formally surrendered.

Final Tally

In the weeks and months prior to and then following the German surrender and the end of World War II, the Nazi extermination camps were discovered one by one. The reaction of those who saw them firsthand was invariably the same—utter disbelief. In spite of all the rumors about their existence and the years of merciless oppression endured by Jews, many people simply could not believe the camps truly existed. Several camps had been hastily abandoned and dismantled by fleeing Nazis to conceal their purpose, but others had not. In early April 1945, for example, members of an American armored division stumbled upon the Ohrdruf camp in central Germany and found piles of corpses as well as hundreds of starving inmates. A few days later a second camp was discovered in the nearby town of Nordhausen.

It contained seven hundred living prisoners along with more than three thousand unburied bodies. The living were barely able to move after months of starvation and torture.

It is impossible to calculate the precise number murdered by Hitler and his Nazi followers during their relentless crusade of terror against the Jews of Europe. Rough estimates, however, suggest anywhere from 5 to 7 million. (More than a million prisoners were killed in the Auschwitz-Birkenau death camp alone.)

Upon visiting the Ohrdruf camp to see it for himself, American general Dwight D. Eisenhower (later president of the United States) wrote in a message to government leaders in Washington, "We are constantly finding German camps in which they have placed political prisoners where unspeakable conditions exist. From my own personal observation, I can state unequivocally that all written statements up to now do not paint the full horrors."

Five

Yesterday, Today, and Tomorrow

IN 2038 THE ONE HUNDREDTH ANNIVERSARY of Kristall-nacht will be observed—a full century after the terroristic explosion that foreshadowed one of the darkest periods in world history. In spite of all the time that has passed, the sting of Kristallnacht and the broader persecution of Jews that followed is still felt by many around the world. What did we learn from it? What has changed as a result of the pogrom and ensuing genocide and, perhaps more important, what hasn't?

On a material level, of the hundreds of synagogues that were destroyed on Kristallnacht, most were never rebuilt, and the sites on which they stood have since been repurposed. The need to rebuild them was of course diminished as a result of Nazi actions. Sadder than the loss of the buildings themselves was the destruction of their contents, much of which was priceless, ancient, and consequently irreplaceable. A few synagogues, however, have been restored, and rebuilding projects continue to this day. As far as Jewish homes, businesses, and other possessions are concerned, the situation is just as grim—since the great majority of Jews either fled or died in the camps, those who benefitted from their losses have never been brought to justice. Relatives of slain Jews have tried in vain to either retrieve stolen items or receive some kind of reparations, but most efforts have been fruitless. The Nazis stole billions from Jewish citizens, and it is likely that they will never be penalized.

On the political front Kristallnacht and the events that followed taught the world a clear moral lesson—that giving a bully what he wants only encourages him to bully more. While it is understandable that France's and Britain's hesitation to confront Hitler came in large part from wanting to avoid potentially costly military action, particularly in the wake of the devastating effects of both World War I and the Great Depression, their policy of appeasement could only have been looked upon by Hitler as a golden opportunity. Even today, with the benefit of historical perspective, it is stunning to think there was any world leader who was willing to enter into a relationship with Hitler after he published *Mein Kampf*, making his view of the Jewish community plain for all the world to see. How many lives would have been spared if Hitler had been taken to task for his stated beliefs long before he took the reins of power?

Along similar lines, how was it possible that millions did not foresee the horrors that awaited Jews (and anyone else the Nazis deemed unsuitable for German society) after the unbridled violence of Kristallnacht? The mere fact that Hitler and his henchmen were willing to resort to such brutality—and then follow it up with more in the weeks and months that followed—should have foreshadowed that

Hitler would not rest until every last undesirable was subtracted from the population. As soon as it became clear other nations could not or would not absorb the full balance of Germany's Jewish population, Hitler had his followers extract them from towns and cities and herd them into concentration camps and ghettos. What further step could he possibly take aside from mass extermination?

A second political lesson is that all those in high positions need to be judged by their actions as well as their words. Hitler was a dazzling public speaker, able to send a crowd of thousands into a frenzy of nationalistic euphoria—and he knew how to use this gift to manipulate and deceive. He promised the German people all manner of things but was vague in his speeches concerning his plans for the Jewish people. It also cannot be forgotten that, in spite of his ruthless tactics, Hitler became Germany's chancellor in January 1933 through completely legal means; his powers of persuasion were unmatched even in the smoke-and-mirrors world of politics. This is not to say that anyone with excellent public-speaking skills is a con artist but that it is important to have evidence that what he or she *does* is equal to what is said.

Hitler knew how to utilize the media to persuade and control the public, so much so that millions in Germany looked upon him as a kind of savior. Political propaganda can be frightfully dangerous in that while it has the power to educate and enlighten, it also has the power to mislead. Hitler's most valuable henchman in this respect was Joseph Goebbels. Goebbels knew how to use film, newspapers, and radio, to make sure the public thought exactly what he and Hitler wanted them to think. He was a utilizer of the "big lie" technique, which is built on the idea that a lie of large enough size, told often enough, will eventually be perceived as fact. Even at the end of the Third Reich, the lies kept coming—on May 1, 1945, the day after Hitler had committed suicide, a radio report was issued stating that "our Führer, Adolf Hitler, fell at his command post in the Reich Chancellery, fighting against Bolshevism to his last breath." At that point Bolshevism had a dual meaning—the communist Russians, who had penetrated Berlin and were moving quickly toward Hitler's bunker, and the Jews, who had supposedly played a key role in the communist movement and sold out Germany during World War I. In Berlin's street even children were urged to continue the streetfighting against the advancing Russian army, risking their young lives to honor their "brave" leader.

Hitler preyed on the desperation of the German people following World War I as they suffered under the terms of the Treaty of Versailles, which left them with damaged pride, a depleted military, and a gasping economy. The German people wanted a national revival at any price, and Hitler knew how to use this to his advantage. Scholars and political analysts have since learned to recognize this pattern: when a society becomes desperate and vulnerable, the opportunists will inevitably emerge. But it is not always possible to warn people away from these types. Tumultuous change in a society can lead to great things or great horrors, and when the masses suffer for long enough, anything is possible.

From November 1945 to October 1946 a variety of Nazi officials were tried in a series of legal proceedings known as the Nuremberg Trials (so named because they were held in the German city of Nuremberg). They were known to be important figures within the Nazi Party, most with a close, personal relationship with Hitler himself. Nevertheless, to the very end they either maintained their innocence or justified their actions by painting themselves as loyal followers, as if they were to be commended for their behavior. Thousands of others took the same approach and simply went on with their lives.

Nazi officials at the Nuremberg Trials listen to the proceedings for their crimes against humanity.

The legacy left behind for the German people is a mighty burden that is felt to this day. It is not uncommon for German television to run documentaries on the Nazi atrocities, and they no doubt serve as a grim reminder. Those of Hitler's generation are either gone now or are in the twilight of their lives, but their children and grandchildren have had to suffer the humiliation of the past. But how does one step away from a shadow when that shadow is of such an immense size?

If there is one bright spot, it is that the Jewish population in Germany is increasing again. Jews are emigrating from countries all over the globe, hoping that they will benefit from a new age, mentality, and government that is trying to atone for its clouded history.

Perhaps both Jews and non-Jews will learn from the past rather than repeat it. When latent prejudice is fueled by unchecked power, the results are usually tragic. Adolf Hitler and the Nazi Party taught us this—at a price of more than 12 million dead, including Jews and other "undesirables," plus the millions of soldiers killed on both sides of the war.

When it was decided in 1989 that the Berlin Wall was to be demolished, the date chosen was November 9—the anniversary of the pogrom. The wall was originally built in 1961 to separate East and West Germany—the former under communist control, the latter under capitalist control—but it acted more as a symbol of the many things that divided the German people above and beyond politics. With the lessons of history well in hand, perhaps we can put to rest strife and discord and work toward a future that promises hope for everyone.

East German border guards demolish a section of the Berlin Wall in November 1989.

In the meantime, perhaps these two words, which are carved in bold capital letters on a plaque at one of the German synagogues that was rebuilt after Kristallnacht, should serve as our guide: *Never Forget*.

Timeline

1889   Adolf Hitler is born April 20 in Braunau am Inn, Austria-Hungary, the fourth of six children.

1907   Hitler moves to Vienna, where he is exposed to rampant anti-Semitism.

1914   Archduke Franz Ferdinand is assassinated by Serbian student Gavrilo Princip in Sarajevo; Austria-Hungary formally declares war on Serbia, marking the start of World War I; Hitler joins a Bavarian unit and goes on to win several citations for bravery.

1918   An armistice is signed, marking the end of World War I.

1919   Germany is forced to sign the humiliating Treaty of Versailles; Hitler joins the German Workers' Party, which eventually changes its name to the National Socialist German Workers' Party, or Nazis.

1923   Hitler, the Nazi leader, attempts to overthrow the German government in the Beer Hall Putsch. The attempt fails, and Hitler and others are sent to prison. While there, he begins writing his book, *Mein Kampf*.

1925–1926   The first and second volumes of *Mein Kampf* are published.

1933   German president Paul von Hindenburg appoints Hitler chancellor in January; in April the first public action against German Jews by Hitler and the Nazis is made.

1934   Hitler becomes Germany's supreme ruler, or führer.

1935   Hitler enacts more anti-Semitic laws, which become known as the Nuremberg Laws.

1938   Jewish immigrant Herschel Grynszpan shoots Nazi Ernst vom Rath, setting off Kristallnacht.

1939   Hitler's military begins its invasion of Poland, sparking the outbreak of World War II.

1941   Several ghettos are established, mostly throughout Poland, to contain and isolate deported Jews under Hitler's governance.

1942   The Nazis establish and begin using extermination camps to systematically murder Jews.

1945   Hitler commits suicide. On May 7 Germany formally surrenders, ending its role in World War II. Remaining extermination and concentration camps are liberated shortly thereafter.

Notes

Chapter One

p. 14, "It was not until I was fourteen or fifteen years old . . .": Adolf Hitler and James Vincent Murphy (translator), *Mein Kampf*. Amsterdam, The Netherlands: Fredonia Classics, 2003, p. 49.

p. 15, ". . . must be accounted as filth . . .": Martin Luther, *The Jews and Their Lies*. Reedy, WV: Liberty Bell, 2004, p. 34.

p. 18, "What soon gave me cause for very serious consideration . . .": Hitler and Murphy, p. 53.

p. 27, "In tireless effort, always ready to help . . .": Albert H. Friedlander, *Out of the Whirlwind: A Reader of Holocaust Literature*. New York: Union for Reform Judaism, 1999, p. 129.

p. 28, ". . . the Jews are the enemies of the New Germany . . .": Melita Maschmann, *Account Rendered: A Dossier on My Former Self*. New York: Abelard-Schuman, 1965, p. 127.

Chapter Two

p. 32, "'You have undoubtedly heard of our great misfortune . . .'": Bertie Grynszpan, quoted in Anthony Read and David Fisher, *Kristallnacht: The Nazi Night of Terror*. New York: Times Books, 1989, pp. 39–40.

p. 45, "'I was summoned from the dais to read a passage . . .'": Quoted in Rita Thalmann and Emmanuel Feinermann, *Crystal Night: 9–10 November 1938*. New York: Holocaust Library, 1974, p. 76.

p. 47, "'The next day I met a friend and we went up to the synagogue. . . .'": Quoted in Martin Gilbert, *Kristallnacht: Prelude to Destruction*. New York: HarperCollins, 2006, p. 36.

Chapter Three

p. 49, "the cowed middle class stared at the Nazi monster . . .": Hans B. Gisevius, *To the Bitter End: An Insider's Account of the Plot to Kill Hitler, 1933–1944*. Da Capo Press: New York, 1998, p. 334.

p. 50, "'I remember the Reichkristallnacht well. . . .'": Quoted in Read and Fisher, p. 123.

p. 51, "'Houses of worship, sacred to others, have been burned down . . .'": Julius von Jan, quoted in Read and Fisher, p. 123.

p. 51, "Ordinary citizens followed the Party's lead in many places . . .": Ian Kershaw, *Hitler: 1936–1945 Nemesis*. New York: W.W. Norton and Company, 2000, p. 344.

p. 54, "'That's the right way to do it . . .'": Quoted in Read and Fisher, p. 125.

p. 56, "Jews Are Beaten, Furniture and Goods Flung From Homes . . .": *The New York Times*, November 11, 1938, front page.

p. 56, "'These men are building their own condemnation . . .'": Herbert Hoover, quoted in Alfred J. Kolatch, *Great Jewish Quotations*. Middle Village, NY: Jonathan David Publishers, 1996, p. 213.

p. 57, "'Not since the days of medieval barbarism . . .'":
Thomas E. Dewey, quoted in Read and Fisher, p. 151.

p. 57, "'make a profit for itself . . .'": Quoted in Rafael
Medoff, "Kristallnacht and the World's Response," in
Holocaust Studies. http://www.aish.com/holocaust/issues/
Kristallnacht_And_The_Worlds_Response.asp.

Chapter Four

p. 69, "'There are some Jews who don't look Jewish who
plonk themselves down . . .'": Joseph Goebbels, quoted
in Thalmann and Feinermann, p. 97.

p. 71, "'We would like the whole world to become so friendly
to the Jews . . .'": Joseph Goebbels, quoted in Read and
Fisher, p. 181.

p. 74, "The annihilation of the Jewish race . . .": Adolf Hitler
and Norman Hepburn Baynes (editor), *The Speeches of
Adolf Hitler: Representative Passages from the Early Speeches,
1922–1924, and Other Selections*. New York: Howard Fertig,
2006, p. 737.

p. 83, "'Dentists hammered out gold teeth, bridges and
crowns . . .'": Quoted in Roderick Stackelberg, *The Nazi
Germany Sourcebook: An Anthology of Texts*. New York:
Routledge, 2002, p. 313.

p. 87, "'We are constantly finding German camps in which
they have placed political prisoners . . .'": Dwight
D. Eisenhower, quoted in University of San Diego,
"Liberation of the Nazi Concentration Camps 1933–
1945" in *World War II Timeline*. http://history.sandiego.
edu/gen/WW2Timeline/.

Chapter Five

p. 91, "'Our Führer, Adolf Hitler, fell at his command post in the Reich Chancellery . . .'": Quoted in Saul Friedländer, *Nazi Germany and the Jews, 1939–1945: The Years of Extermination*. New York: HarperCollins, 2007, p. 661.

Further Information

Books

Altman, Linda Jacobs. *Adolf Hitler: Evil Mastermind of the Holocaust* (Holocaust Heroes and Nazi Criminals). Berkeley Heights, NJ: Enslow Publishers, 2005.

Bard, Mitchell G. *48 Hours of Kristallnacht: Night of Destruction / Dawn of the Holocaust.* Guilford, CT: The Lyons Press, 2008.

Bartel, Judy. *The Holocaust: A Primary Source History* (In Their Own Words). Strongsville, OH: Gareth Stevens Publishing, 2005.

Boas, Jacob. *We Are Witnesses: Five Diaries of Teenagers Who Died in the Holocaust.* New York: Square Fish, 2009.

Downing, David. *Origins of the Holocaust* (World Almanac Library of the Holocaust). Strongsville, OH: World Almanac Education, 2006.

————. *Persecution and Emigration* (World Almanac Library of the Holocaust). Strongsville, OH: World Almanac Education, 2005.

Video/DVDs

The American Experience: America and the Holocaust. WGBH, Boston, 2005.

Auschwitz: Inside the Nazi State. BBC Warner, 2005.

Holocaust: Dachau and Sachsenhausen. Arts Magic, 2006.

The Nazis: A Warning from History. BBC Warner, 2005.

Websites

America and the Holocaust
www.pbs.org/wgbh/amex/holocaust/
PBS's site dedicated to the study and discussion of the Holocaust from an American perspective.

Holocaust Studies
www.aish.com/holocaust/default.asp
This website offers information about the Nazi persecution of the Jews, including several pages on Kristallnacht.

Museum of Tolerance
motlc.wiesenthal.com/site/pp.asp?c=gvKVLcMVIuG&b=394679
Kristallnacht page from the Simon Wiesenthal Center and Museum of Tolerance. Has links to many other excellent pages of interest.

The Rise of Adolf Hitler
www.historyplace.com/worldwar2/riseofhitler/index.htm
History Place pages about the rise of Adolf Hitler. Vital for understanding how he rose to power.

United States Holocaust Memorial Museum
www.ushmm.org/
American online museum about the Holocaust. Loads of information available in several languages and many useful links.

Bibliography

Books

Friedlander, Albert H. *Out of the Whirlwind: A Reader of Holocaust Literature*. New York: Union for Reform Judaism, 1999.

Friedländer, Saul. *Nazi Germany and the Jews, Volume I: The Years of Persecution, 1933–1939*. New York: HarperCollins, 1997.

———. *Nazi Germany and the Jews, 1939–1945: The Years of Extermination*. New York: HarperCollins, 2007.

Gilbert, Martin. *Kristallnacht: Prelude to Destruction*. New York: HarperCollins, 2006.

Gisevius, Hans B. *To the Bitter End: An Insider's Account of the Plot to Kill Hitler, 1933–1944*. Da Capo Press: New York, 1998.

Hitler, Adolf, and Norman Hepburn Baynes (editor). *The Speeches of Adolf Hitler: Representative Passages from the Early Speeches, 1922–1924, and Other Selections*. New York: Howard Fertig, 2006.

———, and James Vincent Murphy (translator). *Mein Kampf*. Amsterdam, The Netherlands: Fredonia Classics, 2003.

Johnson, Eric A. *Nazi Terror: The Gestapo, Jews, and Ordinary Germans*. New York: Basic Books, 1999.

Kershaw, Ian. *Hitler: 1936–1945 Nemesis*. New York: W.W. Norton and Company, 2000.

Kolatch, Alfred J. *Great Jewish Quotations*. Middle Village, NY: Jonathan David Publishers, 1996.

Luther, Martin. *The Jews and Their Lies*. Reedy, WV: Liberty Bell, 2004.

Maschmann, Melita. *Account Rendered: A Dossier on My Former Self*. New York: Abelard-Schuman, 1965.

Medoff, Rafael. "Kristallnacht and the World's Response," in 'Holocaust Studies.' http://www.aish.com/holocaust/issues/Kristallnacht_And_The_Worlds_Response.asp.

Mosse, George L. *The Crisis of German Ideology: Intellectual Origins of the Third Reich*. New York: Grossett & Dunlap, 1964.

Peukert, Detlev J. K. *Inside Nazi Germany: Conformity, Opposition, and Racism in Everyday Life*. New Haven, CT: Yale University Press, 1987.

Read, Anthony, and David Fisher. *Kristallnacht: The Nazi Night of Terror*. New York: Times Books, 1989.

Shirer, William L. *The Rise and Fall of the Third Reich: A History of Nazi Germany*. New York: Simon & Schuster, 1960.

Stackelberg, Roderick. *The Nazi Germany Sourcebook: An Anthology of Texts*. New York: Routledge, 2002.

Thalmann, Rita, and Emmanuel Feinermann. *Crystal Night: 9–10 November 1938*. New York: Holocaust Library, 1974.

University of San Diego. "Liberation of the Nazi Concentration Camps 1933–1945" in 'World War II Timeline.' http://history.sandiego.edu/gen/WW2Timeline/.

Index

Page numbers in **boldface** are illustrations.

About the Author

WIL MARA is an award-winning novelist and author of more than one hundred books. He has written many educational titles for young readers, covering such subjects as history, geography, sports, science, and nature, plus several biographies. More information about his work can be found at www.wilmara.com.